A COMPARISON OF SPORT AND MILITARY LEADERS

A dissertation submitted to
the faculty of the United States Sports Academy
in partial fulfillment of the requirements
for the degree of

Doctor of Education
In
Sport Management

by
Christopher P. Johnson
Chair: Dr. Bret Simmermacher
Daphne, Alabama
June 2018

DEDICATION

For mom and dad. Something tells me that if the two of you were here, you would not be surprised that I am about to complete my doctorate.

ACKNOWLEDGEMENTS

"It takes a village to raise a child" and the same can be said for undertaking a doctoral dissertation. This entire experience would not be possible without the help of some very talented and special people. There are many people who I must acknowledge for their contributions to this study.

First, I would like to acknowledge my dissertation committee, Dr. Bret Simmermacher, Dr. Stephen Butler, and Dr. Fred Cromartie; especially my dissertation committee chair Dr. Bret Simmermacher for his endless pursuit of excellence as well as military and leadership knowledge that vastly improved this study.

At home, I would like to mention my officer candidate school for answering countless questions regarding the military. From our TAC staff exemplifying the highest standard of leadership to my fellow officer candidates who were there to answer all my questions, this project would not be possible without your eager willingness to help. I also need to personally acknowledge the faculty in the Lasell College Sports Management department including Dr. William Nowlan and Dr. Daniel Sargeant for their willingness to answer any question regarding research that crossed my mind and adding me to their team, allowing me to lead my own team of students. Correspondingly, I would like to thank all the research participants, the sports and military leaders who participated in the study as well as Dr. Jean Côté for allowing me to use her Coaching Behaviour Scale for Sports (CBS-S). It is because of you all, that I believe this study is complete. The value you are adding to the domain of team leadership will stem through generations.

Finally, I would like to thank my wife Stephanie for providing me with love and support throughout this process. Regardless of how crazy my ideas appear; from starting businesses to enrolling as a doctoral and officer candidate at the same time, she always supports them in the end.

TABLE OF CONTENTS

LIST OF TABLES

ABSTRACT

Johnson, C. Degree: Doctor of Education in Sports Management, United States Sports Academy. June 2018. Title: *A Comparison of Sport and Military Leaders.* Chair: Dr. Bret Simmermacher.

This study provides leaders from diverse backgrounds with a comprehensive overview of existing research of leadership between sport and military leaders. Sports and the military are industries where leadership is applied over a wide range of diverse and dynamic situations. By comparing athletes' and military personnel's views on their leaders' leadership style effectiveness, it provided insight that can be carried to other domains. The results of the Coaching Behaviour Scale for Sports CBS-S study instrument were analyzed and interpreted to determine which characteristics are most similar between the 2 industries.

CHAPTER I

INTRODUCTION

Leadership is the foremost force guiding teams. For this reason, mastering the process of leadership has been the primary objective of people in positions of authority for as long as people have formed teams. History has painted an image of leaders as semi-divine individuals yielding the gift of charisma and oration as they move up the ladder influencing people exponentially while gaining power as their reach spreads. Traditionally, there was a craftsmanship behind leadership, allowing leaders to create bonds over years of participating in an industry, building connections, and gaining influence that allowed them to identify themselves as business, medical, political, or educational leaders. However, industry is changing and people in leadership positions are jumping between organizations or combining efforts between merging industries where their clout in decisions is not nearly as influencing.

Leadership is changing from a position of established trust over years of relationship building to a role as a team builder empowering newly formed or adopted teams to make connections and team-centric decisions within a short period of time. With this said, identifying specific leadership characteristics that hold true between industries, is of significance to the modern leader. Identifying what allows successful leaders to influence diverse populations, with frequently adjusting members to work effectively towards a goal, is the key to mastering the process of leadership in today's dynamic and rapidly evolving environment.

Background of the Problem

Collinson and Tourish (2015) suggested that leadership has been traditionally taught with a romanticized hero approach focusing on charisma as a necessary component to success and power as an almost tangible natural resource rather than a force influenced by emotions and politics. It is of significance that elements of leadership, such as charisma, are not reserved for the few who naturally possess a specific blend of inheritable and unalterable traits. Steve Jobs, former Chief Executive Officer (CEO) and founder of Apple, learned through experience how to be more charismatic. Early interviews with Mr. Jobs, from the 1990s, show his lacking charisma; however, as time progressed, he became one of the most charismatic leaders in modern society (McKay & McKay, 2014). Being a leader is not as simple as putting on a mask and cape and instantly transforming into a master of leadership in one's given field. Part of what the researcher intended to clarify is leadership as a dynamic and integrated process with learnable characteristics rather than an isolated system with traits specific to every industry and led by a lucky few with the natural gift of charisma.

Leadership is a naturally occurring and ever-evolving process, adjusting as the situation dictates. Understanding the environment and role leaders and followers play in their dynamic situation is essential to understanding the mechanisms of leadership. Leadership is as dynamic as the people composing the teams and influence is as variable and fluid as the diverse group of followers. As society grows, industries such as sports, the military, business, medicine, politics, and education must consider an ever-larger group of differing individuals. To effectively lead such a diverse population, leaders need to possess specific leadership characteristics that are effective among diverse populations and varying environments. Leadership is not an autonomous sport, but rather a delicate exchange between leader and follower influence.

Statement of the Problem

The purpose of this study was to compare the similarities and differences in leadership styles between sport and military leaders. There has been a long-time link between sports and the military. William James (2015) in his work *The Moral Equivalent of War*, as well as Chris Hedges' (2002) work *War is a Force That Gives us Meaning*, both highlighted the notion that sports unleash a higher state of being in people. War, in all its death and destruction, enables higher qualities of people such as discipline, courage, self-sacrifice, purpose, meaning, and a reason for living. Dr. Steve Taylor (2014) believed sports satisfy these virtues. Based on the current literature, it appears that most of the psychological and sociological effects of warfare can be replicated in sport. In Karl Marlantes (2011) novel *What It is Like To Go To War*, the author mentioned aggression is an innate trait, which in certain instances can manifest itself in war. He believes soldiers transcend into being part of something bigger than themselves.

Sport and the military have a long intertwined relationship. Although documentation is scarce, there is growing evidence of sports having been used as a form of military training in ancient China to strengthen and discipline soldiers through wrestling, fencing, hunting, and swimming among other events (Fried, 2012). Furthermore, some of the first institutions to make sport a major part of student life were military academies under General Wellington's belief that "battles were won and lost on the playing fields of youth. The better the sports program, they reasoned, the better the soldier" (Stark, 2010). It was even said that Stephan Crane had no trouble writing *The*

Red Badge of Courage, because although he had never been to war, he was coaching and playing football while completing his manuscript (Burton, 2010). Mr. Crane could transfer his football experience to the battlefield. In Mark Edmundson's book, *Why Football Matters* (2015), he made many comparisons between football and life that could be made between the military and life. The similarities between Dr. Edmundson's lessons about character, losing, channeling emotion, faith, compassion, and courage learned from football are comparable to those learned in the military. History provides a strong link between sports and the military giving reason to search for underlying leadership characteristics.

Moreover, sports and the military are two industries composed of diverse individuals from around the planet. Each sport has its own sub-culture consisting of people merging their cultural traditions with them as they join. Research by Salvatore (2014) showed sports' ability to increase collaboration among diverse individuals. In this respect, the military is no different than sports. Every branch of the United States military has its own culture, which is further influenced by occupational differences. President Obama, during his 2016 Veterans Day speech, stated that the U.S. military is the "single most diverse institution in our country" (Rhodan, 2016). When examining diverse industries that join to accomplish great achievements, sports and the United States military are great industries for examination.

Purpose of the Study

The purpose of this study was to examine the similarities and differences in leadership styles between sport and military personnel.

Research Questions

The following research questions guided this study:

RQ1: How do athletes and military personnel rate their leaders in physical training and planning?

RQ2: How do athletes and military personnel rate their leaders in technical skills?

RQ3: How do athletes and military personnel rate their leaders in mental preparation?

RQ4: How do athletes and military personnel rate their leaders in goal setting?

RQ5: How do athletes and military personnel rate their leaders in personal rapport?

Hypotheses

Ho1: There is not a statistically significant difference between sport and military leadership styles as measured by physical training and planning

Ha1: There is a statistically significant difference between sport and military leadership styles as measured by physical training and planning

Ho2: There is not a statistically significant difference between sport and military leadership styles as measured by technical skills

Ha2: There is a statistically significant difference between sport and military leadership styles as measured by technical skills

Ho3: There is not a statistically significant difference between sport and military leadership styles as measured by mental preparation

Ha3: There is a statistically significant difference between sport and military leadership styles as measured by mental preparation

Ho4: There is not a statistically significant difference between sport and military leadership styles as measured by goal setting

Ha4: There is a statistically significant difference between sport and military leadership styles as measured by goal setting

Ho5: There is not a statistically significant difference between sport and military leadership styles as measured by personal rapport

Ha5: There is a statistically significant difference between sport and military leadership styles as measured by personal rapport.

Significance of the Study

The significance of this study was to identify specific leadership styles that are effective in both the military and in sports settings. Understanding the leadership styles that are effective may enhance the success of coaches at all levels of sports.

Definition of Terms

The following terms are professionally and operationally defined for this study using military and civilian definitions:

Characteristic - A special quality or trait that makes a person, thing, or group different from others (Merriam-Webster).

Cohesion - A condition in which people or things are closely united (Merriam-Webster).

Collaboration - A synergy that occurs when individuals join strengths towards a common goal.

Collective-efficacy - a group's shared belief in its conjoint capabilities to organize and execute the courses of action required to produce given levels of attainments. (Bandura, 1970)

Culture - A way of thinking, behaving, or working that exists in a place or organization (Merriam-Webster).

Direction - Providing clear direction involves communicating what to do to accomplish a mission: prioritizing tasks, assigning responsibility for completion, and ensuring subordinates understand the standard. Although subordinates want and need direction, they expect challenging tasks, quality training, and adequate resources. They should have appropriate freedom of action. Providing clear direction allows followers to adapt to changing circumstances through modifying plans and orders through disciplined initiative within the commander's intent (ADRP 6-22).

Dynamic - Always active or changing (Merriam-Webster).

Efficacy - The power to produce a desired result or effect (Merriam-Webster).

Environment - The conditions and influences that affect the growth, health, progress, etc., of someone or something (Merriam-Webster). Environment includes the place and time leaders and followers interact.

Follower - someone who supports and is guided by another person or by a group, religion, etc. (Merriam-Webster). It is important to note here that a defining role of a follower is to support their leader.

Group – A number of individuals assembled together or having some unifying relationship (Merriam-Webster).

Improve the organization - Improving for the future means capturing and acting on important lessons of ongoing and completed projects and missions. Improving is an act of stewardship, striving to create effective, efficient organizations (ADRP 6-22).

Influencing - Influencing is getting people to do what is required. Influencing entails more than simply passing along orders. Through words and personal example, leaders communicate purpose, direction, and motivation (ADRP 6-22).

Leader – A person who has commanding authority or influence (Merriam-Webster).

Leadership - The process of influencing people by providing purpose, direction, and motivation to accomplish the mission and improve the organization (ADRP 6-22).

Purpose - Purpose gives subordinates the reason to achieve a desired outcome. Leaders should provide clear purpose for their followers (ADRP 6-22).

Motivation - Motivation supplies the will and initiative to do what is necessary to accomplish a mission. Motivation comes from within, but others' actions and words affect it. A leader's role in motivation is to understand the needs and desires of others, to align and elevate individual desires into team goals, and to inspire others to accomplish those larger goals. Some people have high levels of internal motivation to get a job done, while others need more reassurance, positive reinforcement, and feedback. Indirect approaches to motivation can be as successful as direct approaches. Setting a personal example can sustain the drive in others. This becomes apparent when leaders share the hardships (ADRP 6-22).

Situation - All the facts, conditions, and events that affect someone or something at a particular time and in a particular place (Merriam-Webster). This includes leaders, followers, and the environmental context (place and time) as well as any additional influential elements.

Style - A distinctive manner or custom of behaving or conducting oneself (Merriam-Webster).

Team - A group of people who collaborate towards a common goal.

Scope of the Study

This study was a mixed-methods descriptive study of leadership practices throughout sports and the military. The primary research instrument was a detailed valid and reliable tool designed to collect practice demographic information and assess leadership styles among sport and military leaders.

Assumptions

The assumptions of this study were:

1. There are specific leadership characteristics common to both effective military leaders and effective sports leaders.

2. The participants responded honestly and openly to all questions asked.

3. The obtained sample is a fair representation of the overall sport and military leadership populations.

4. The findings can be generalized to universal leadership practices.

5. The valid and reliable survey questions apply to both athletes and military personnel.

Limitations

The limitations of this study were:

1. Representatives of sport and military leaders may not accurately represent leaders from other industries.

2. Representatives of sport and military personnel may provide a description of their leader that differs significantly from how others view that same leader.

3. The degree to which the participants understand the questions is unknown.

4. Respondents of the study may not have answered honestly while evaluating their coach or supervisor without fear of repercussions from above.

Delimitations

The delimitations of this study were:

1. Only two industries were examined. Although sports and the military are diverse industries, they are only two of many possible team cultures.

2. The survey instrument was used to compare leaders from two different fields.

3. The survey instrument used is specifically designed for coaches.

CHAPTER II

REVIEW OF LITERATURE

Introduction

A comprehensive literature review links relationships between various

components, contradictions, and gaps as well as unanswered questions of a topic. This

review of literature used inductive reasoning to establish broad boundaries and work its

way into specifics. Starting with the composition of leadership and team building on a

broad scale with no regard for specific areas such as sport and the military. After

establishing a broad understanding of the topic, an examination of sport and military

leadership and team building was performed, and the results compared and placed into

one of two groups. Group one being overarching leadership characteristics between

sports and the military and group two being leadership and team building characteristics

that were suggested in literature but not identified as common characteristics between

sport and military leadership styles. Findings that appear in group two will still be taken

into consideration when comparing the findings of the literature review to that of the

study instrument.

The research was organized by theme. This was done to determine if there are

specific leadership characteristics occurring between sports and the military. If

characteristics can be identified between sports and the military, they may be universal

across all leadership situations because of the diverse and dynamic nature of sports and

the military. After examining leadership literature with no direct objective of identifying

sport or military leadership, the second theme looked specifically at sports leaders and

how their influence contributes to team success. Upon analyzing sports leadership, military leadership was dissected in the same manner in search of how military leaders influence their subordinates to success. A fourth and final theme examined previous research, which drew common ground regarding sport and military leadership. Literature directly concerned with sport and military leadership built upon previously discovered similarities between sports and military leaders.

Conceptual Framework

A conceptual framework organized by theme was established cataloging how and why leaders in sports and the military lead as they do. The researcher proposed relationships regarding the process for leadership between the two areas.

Review of Research

Innate Versus Learned Behaviors

Research throughout the 20th century viewed leadership as a group of innate traits that great leaders naturally possess. This was known as the trait approach and was the foundation behind how people identified leaders. Famous leaders such as Joan of Arc, Abraham Lincoln, and Napoleon were studied to determine which innate traits made them effective leaders. As time progressed, researchers shifted focus towards skills and abilities of leadership that can be learned and developed. This shift in perspective was made popular by Robert Katz's 1955 Harvard Business Review article, *Skills of an Effective Administrator*. Katz's article changed leadership's focus from innate traits to acquired leadership behaviors (Northouse, 2013).

Research by Bourjade, Thierry, Hausberger, and Petit (2015) on leadership concluded there is no individual leader. Leadership is rather shared; there is no one specific leader. This finding suggests leadership is not fixed, but rather available to those who rise to the occasion. Whoever has the skill and desire to accomplish the job is the one followed. This translates to people as well, success as a leader comes to those with a learning mindset who are inspirers and active role models always improving their skills and knowledge. Although some skills are more innate than others such as competitiveness, achiever mindset, and empathy, traits such as communication can be taught. What they discovered was the key determinant in teaching leadership behaviors is practical leadership experience (Jonathan, 2003; Tillman, 2015). Sport is a practical leadership experience that was found to provide value beyond classroom settings by providing mentors, tools for leadership, image and managing perceptions, and exposure to leadership styles (Harris, 2016).

Joo, Song, Lim, and Yoon (2012) learned creativity has a significant relationship between perceived learning cultures. In return, creativity also enhanced team cohesion, which adds to support structure, acting as a full circle feedback system with team creativity. Creativity is what allows people to learn how to become leaders after initially failing. Kim, Magnusen, and Andrew (2016) proposed that horizontal communication had a significant positive association with both group integration-task and group integration-social meaning when people in a group accept each other they had a higher incidence of team cohesion. Alternatively, when teams did not accept each other they did not work as well. People need to be able to work effectively together if they are to get the most creativity out of their work. Coming together to create something better than what can be achieved alone is a basic principle of nature. According to Jacobs' (2016) TED-Ed presentation, "emergence is a basic property of many complex systems of interacting elements."

In Jacobs' (2016) video he provided an example of schools of fish coming together to improve their overall state through emergence and compares it to billions of neurons firing in the human brain to create people's consciousness. Alone, both the fish and the human brain are not nearly as effective at survival as when they emerge as one. The school of fish and human consciousness are not controlled by any single fish or neuron. They simply emerge if they have the right set of logical values. Leaders are significant contributors to enhancing team cohesion. They are in a sense providing the logic for team members to emerge. Knowing this, the entire process of developing future leaders is affected by the quality of our current leaders. Since future leaders' success is dependent on current mentors' ability to emerge their students in a nurturing leadership development system.

Sport Leadership

Sports are apparent in every society across the world. Cultures are highly influenced by the dominant sports of the area and sports leaders. In the United States, sports are a multi-billion-dollar industry driven towards the desire to win. Beginning with youth sports and the desire for bragging rights all the way up to professional sports' multi-million-dollar player contracts, sports are a victory driven machine (Humphreys & Humphreys, 2008). Successful sports leaders are looked highly upon in American society and discussed on sports television shows regarding the effectiveness of their strategies, decision making, team cohesion, and overall character (Healy, 2015). It is well known that New England Patriots coach Bill Belichick is an effective leader on the field, leading his team to five Super Bowl championships, but not many people know his father Steve Belichick, who was influential in Bill's development as a coach, was himself a coach at the Naval Academy for 30 years as well as a World War II veteran. It was perhaps Bill Belichick's exposure to sports leadership from growing up watching his father coach the Naval Academy that led to his success as a sport leader in his own career.

The survey conducted in this study was an examination into the similarities and differences that exist between sport and military leaders that make their coaching philosophies effective beyond the norm. Such an influential mechanism of influence deserves to be studied for its implications on society. For this study, how athletes and military personnel view a team leader they consider good was cross-examined with military leadership to reveal any overlapping characteristics that can be applied to leadership in other domains.

After a careful examination of the literature, specific leadership characteristics were shown to be more apparent in effective leaders, autocratic behavior, positive personality traits, team cohesion, leads by example, and sense of responsibility. Table 2.1 lists the main sports leadership characteristics on the top row with defining traits that appeared throughout the literature listed below (Caron, Bloom, Loughead, & Hoffman, 2016; Cormier, Bloom, & Harvey, 2015; Filho, Tenenbaum, & Yang, 2015; Harrison & Smith, 2016; Jeffrey, 2012; Mohammadzade, Zardoshtains, & Hossini, 2012):

Table 2. 1: Common Characteristics of Sports Leaders.

Sports Leaders	Autocratic Behavior	Positive Personality Traits	Team Cohesion	Leads by Example	Sense of Responsibility
	Authoritative Behavior	Physical Prowess - Ability	Collective Efficacy	High-Performance Standards	Motivation
	Focus on Training and Instruction	High Work Ethic	Team Mental Models		Support
		Determination			Communication
		Motivation			

Military Leadership

Leadership is the backbone of the military. Yet, as noted by Sir Michael Thomas Howard, the British historian, military leaders may "exercise [the purpose of their profession] only once in a lifetime, if indeed that often" (Maneuver Self Study Program, 2016). Leadership is considered the most dynamic element of combat power, focusing the other elements and acting as a catalyst for success (FM 3-0). Leadership is essential to all Army operations (FM 6-22). Moreover, military leadership is often executed under complex, dynamic, and turbulent environments (Bangari, 2014). With that said, the operating environment of the leader often shapes the demands of the training. Military leaders operate in an ever-changing context that is continuously accelerating pace (Morath, Leonard, & Zaccaro, 2011). This demanding work environment justifies an examination of military leadership for transfer to industries such as business, medicine, politics, and education when times are demanding and effective leadership is essential.

Consequently, an in-depth examination of military leadership characteristics was performed and the following were considered significant to effectively leading military teams (See Table 2.2), professional excellence, well-balanced vision, empathy, and lead by example (Bangari, 2014; Bangari & Prasad, 2012, Boies & Howell, 2009; Govindarajan & Faber, 2016; Harrison & Smith, 2016; Tillman, 2015). Within those four characteristics of military leadership, specific traits were identified as significant. As with sports leaders, the major leadership characteristics and minor defining traits for military leaders are listed in Table 2.2.

Sport and Military Leaders Combined

A survey was delivered to athletes and military personnel asking them questions regarding their respected leader's coaching style. The results of the survey were gathered and analyzed to determine if they support the hypothesis. If there were no overlapping leadership characteristics supporting the hypothesis, then that was analyzed and discussed.

Table 2. 2: Common Characteristics of Military Leaders.

Military Leaders	Professional Excellence	Well-balanced vision	Empathy	Lead by example
	Competence in Team Building	Letting go of values that no longer serve	Impeccable moral integrity	Courageous enough to pursue the right cause
	Self-Efficacy	Managing Present values	Genuine concern for command	Empowering subordinates
	High Performance Standard	Creating and adopting new values	Self-sacrificing for subordinates	Transformational leadership
	Shared Knowledge		Sincerity of Purpose	Team Cohesion
	Coordination		Compassionate approach towards all in general	
	Team Mental Models			
	Interconnected			
	Lead by example			

Conclusion

In closing, sport and military leadership have overlapping areas of interest that may be of significance in domains outside of sports and the military. The students of today are tomorrow's leaders. It is this researcher's hope that the remainder of the research will link sport and military leadership and provide meaningful survey responses to discover specific leadership characteristics that can be used across all industries.

CHAPTER III

METHODOLOGY

Introduction

This chapter discusses the research design and procedures of the study on specific leadership characteristics that are common between sport and military leaders to gain a better understanding of effective leadership characteristics that may be universal between industries, allowing leaders from a variety of backgrounds to more effectively lead and influence their teams. Thus, this chapter provides a detailed discussion of the following components of the study's methodology: (a) selection of the subjects, (b) instrumentation, (c) procedures, (d) research design and data analysis.

Research Objective

This study was intended to identify specific leadership styles that are evident in both military and sports leadership. Sport and military leaders were chosen for this study because of their diverse populations and variety of sub-cultures within their domains.

Selection of the Subjects

The researcher surveyed athletes and military personnel. The respondents underwent a demographic questionnaire related to their personal and professional backgrounds to gain a greater understanding of their history. The respective athletes or military personnel answered questions on the Coaching Behaviour Scale for Sports (CBS-S) created by Dr. Jean Côté, to identify their coaches' or military supervisors' leadership behavior. Athletes were classified as such by being an athlete who currently or previously participated in sports under a coach's guidance and military personnel were classified as such by being a current or past member of the United States Military.

Recruitment

Recruitment was done through the researcher's professional sport and military network. The researcher is currently active in the sport and military profession and has a vast network to reach out to. The researcher requested fellow professionals in the sport and military field who met the specified qualifications mentioned in the Selection of the Subjects section of this study to participate in the CBS-S. Once an individual either personally volunteered for the study or provided contact information for another individual who fit the criteria, contact was made with that individual through the platform that was provided. Because this study was done through the researcher's professional network, emails, facebook.com, and linkedin.com were used to reach out to the public for volunteers, but the researcher did not personally ask a specific individual to volunteer. Once an individual volunteered or was recommended to the researcher, initial and follow-up emails and phone calls were sent out to encourage participation.

The researcher chose this method for communication with participants because social media such as facebook.com as well as other social media networks provide a vast reach throughout sport and the military. A survey distributed using SurveyMonkey with the demographic questionnaire and CBS-S was sent to the athletes and military personnel. An appendix includes the survey as well as the facebook.com, linkedin.com post, and emails sent to the researcher's network.

Instrumentation

The CBS-S is the questionnaire. It consists of 47 questions divided into seven areas regarding how often specific coaching behaviors are experienced. The instrument was developed by Dr. Jean Côté and permission to use the instrument for this study was granted by Dr. Côté. The significance of the coaching behaviors experienced by the participants was identified and a comparison was made between athletes and military personnel.

To estimate the reliability of the CBS-S instrument for research, an examination of Côté et al.'s (1999), study *An Exploratory Examination of the Coaching Behaviour Scale for Sport* was examined. The study showed the reliability of the CBS-S, which performed an exploratory factor analysis with 205 athletes, determining the CBS-S can be used as a research tool to provide new and insightful data about coaches' behaviors.

This research provided evidence that the CBS-S has an acceptable degree of rigor in a number of key psychometric properties. First, the findings conform to the qualitative studies upon which it was based, which provided external validity. Second, the study's construct represents a wide range of variability, indicating it captures a wide range of coaching behaviors across a variety of sports. Third, the constructs possess reasonable validity (factor and discriminant) and reliability (internal consistency and test-retest reliability). These results indicate that the CBS-S is a reliable instrument for analyzing theoretical and applied coaching behaviors.

Demographic Information

All athletes and military personnel participating in the survey are evaluating their leaders based upon the questions of the CBS-S. Participants were asked to partake in a demographic questionnaire prior to the interview questions to gain a better understanding of the participant. The demographic questionnaire measured background statistics on the participants; identified the athletes' primary sport, which branch of the military that the military personnel were associated with, and what is their highest rank. In general, how satisfied or dissatisfied are they with their life, what their highest level of education, and what if any was their main area of study in school. All questions requested participants to circle the most appropriate response. It is to be noted that the demographic questionnaire is independent from the CBS-S and was developed by the researcher and not Dr. Côté.

Procedures

Research participants were recruited from their respective fields in sports and the military. They were recruited by reaching out to the researcher's professional social network, the United States Sports Academy alumni page, and the National Association of Collegiate Directors of Athletics (NACDA). An attempt will be made to include a diverse background of sports and branches of the military.

When participants received their survey, they were immediately told they were participating in a questionnaire that, with their consent, will be recorded to help identify common leadership styles between sport and military leaders. The researcher then went over their informed consent form asking them if there is anything they need clarified. A copy of the informed consent form is included in Appendix A.

During the first part of the study, sport and military leaders completed a short demographic questionnaire, asking them questions related to their experience in their respective fields. This portion of the study takes less than five minutes. Any clarification regarding questions was made available. The purpose of the demographic section is so the researcher could later divide the data into various data groups based on demographic information gathered from the survey.

Upon completing the demographic section, the athletes and military personnel were directed to the survey questions. These questions were designed to gain insight into participants' perspective regarding the behaviors of their leaders. Participants were instructed to take their time answering the questions and if an idea regarding a previously answered question manifests in their mind at a later point during the interview, they were allowed to go back and change their answers. When the researcher answered the study questions, the process took five minutes. Participants were told the interview process should take less than 10 minutes to complete.

Once the survey was complete, the participants were asked if there is anything further they would like to add to their responses. Once they were finished, they were reminded that they may be contacted again later to clarify any questions the interviewer may have regarding their survey.

Research Design and Data Analysis

In-Depth Close-Ended Survey

An in-depth close-ended survey, the CBS-S, was used to gather data on sport leader athletes' and military subordinates' leadership behavior experience. The CBS-S consists of 47 questions rated on a 1-7 Likert Scale with a response of one meaning never and a response of seven meaning always.

By allowing participants to take a quantitative close-ended survey, it allowed them to rank the emotions they experience with their sport or military leader in seven different categories; physical training and planning, technical skills, mental preparation, goal setting, competition strategies, personal rapport, and negative personal rapport. This allowed the researcher to compare results from sports and the military without any industry jargon interfering. The CBS-S was administered to a minimum of 50 athletes and 50 military personnel. The researcher contacted the athlete and military personnel through the procedures mentioned in the recruitment section of this paper.

Data Analysis

The CBS-S examined seven different constructs, physical training and planning, technical skills, mental preparation, goal setting, competition strategies, personal rapport, and negative personal rapport. Data were gathered, and a comparison was made between sports and military participants concerning each category. Subsequent to collecting the survey data, data were analyzed by the researcher using the independent sample *t-test* of data analysis against Chapter II's literature review findings to determine if any correlations could be made between the findings from the CBS-S and previous literature. Responses from the CBS-S identifying specific coaching behaviors as positively correlated between sport and military leaders were identified as such and labeled as specific common leadership styles between sport and military leaders.

Summary

The purpose of this study was to determine if there were specific leadership styles that can be identified from studying sport and military leaders. Specifically, if there are common leadership styles between the diverse fields of sport and the military. This study was conducted through an on-line survey. Sport and military professionals were contacted through social networking websites and email requesting if they themselves are or someone they know is a sport and / or military leader willing to participate in the study. The responses were analyzed to determine positively correlated responses that can be identified as common leadership styles between sport and military leaders.

CHAPTER IV

RESULTS

Introduction

The previous chapters have detailed the background and literature review of this doctoral study, reviewed the relevant literature, and detailed the methodology of the study. In Chapter IV, the researcher portrayed the data as obtained through the following methodology outlined in Chapter III.

The purpose of this study was to address the following, "examine the similarities and differences in leadership styles between sport and military personnel?" Therefore, the researcher used this study to discover any significant relationship that existed between sport leaders and military leaders. The research questions for this study were as follows:

1. How do athletes and military personnel rate their leaders in physical training and planning?

2. How do athletes and military personnel rate their leaders in technical skills?

3. How do athletes and military personnel rate their leaders in mental preparation?

4. How do athletes and military personnel rate their leaders in goal setting?

5. How do athletes and military personnel rate their leaders in personal rapport?

Demographics

The researcher e-mailed and posted a letter on social networks where he has connections to sport and military groups. The researcher sent the first letter on April 15, 2018 and closed the study on May 23, 2018. Participants completed a total of 95 surveys representing 16 sports and all five branches of the military. Of those surveys, 64 were analyzed (athlete =40, military = 24) as some of the surveys submitted provided incomplete data.

The researcher did not ask the athletes and military personnel participating to complete the survey. Instead, the athletes and military personnel volunteered to complete a survey consisting of the following: (1) a rater version of the CBS-S and (2) a demographic survey. The CBS-S consisted of 47 items rating the athlete's and military personnel's perception of their leader as a coach in seven areas. Five of those areas were analyzed for the purpose of this study.

Athlete or Military Personnel

A summary of the distribution of participants that were athletes or military personnel is in table 4.1.

Table 4. 1: Athlete or Military Personnel.

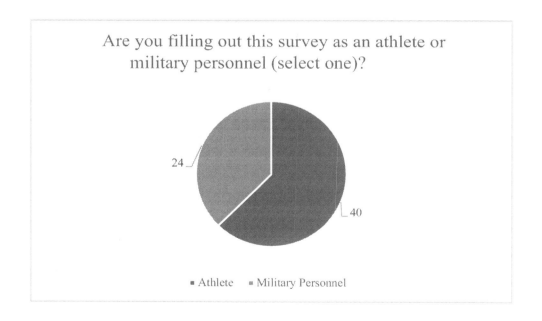

Age

The significant age range was 18 through 69 years old. The number of participants in the age range of 50-59 and 60-69 was much smaller with the largest group being 19-29 years old. Table 4.2 summarizes the participant age.

Table 4. 2: Age Distribution of Participants.

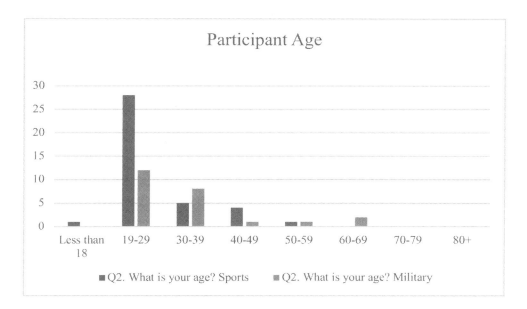

Athlete's Primary Sport

The category with the highest number was American Soccer with 10 participants representing 6.2% of the participants. Four participants are in the track and field category, three in swimming, and there is a five-way tie with two participants each in American football, basketball, cross country, field hockey, and tennis. Table 4.3 summarizes the athlete's primary sport.

Table 4. 3: Athlete's Primary Sport Distribution of Participants.

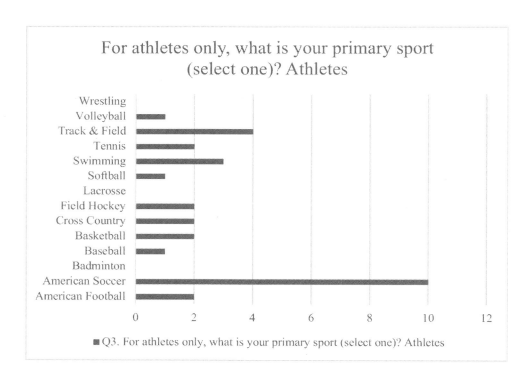

Table 4.3. Athlete's Primary Sport Distribution of Participants

Military Branch

Participants came from three branches of the military, the Army, Navy, and Marine Corps. The category with the most participants was the Army with a total of 19 individuals. Marine Corps was next with a total of four individuals, followed by the Navy with one individual. Coast Guard and Air Force participants did not complete the study and thus their responses were not used.

Table 4.4 summarizes the branches of the military which individuals represent.

Table 4. 4: Military Branch Distribution of Participants.

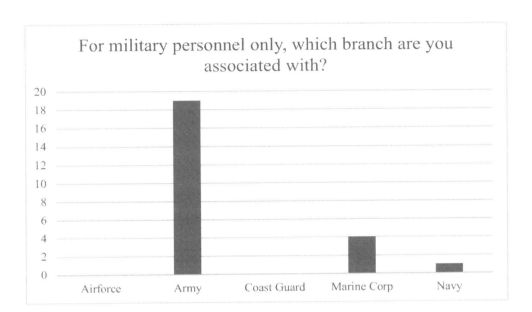

Military Rank

Military personnel's ranks represent a wide spectrum of enlisted, non-commissioned officers, and commissioned officers. The category with the most participants was commissioned officer with a total of 11 individuals. Junior enlisted was next with a total of seven individuals. The final category was senior enlisted (NCO) with five individuals. Warrant officer had a total of one response.

Table 4.5 summarizes the ranks of individuals in the study.

Table 4. 5: Military Rank Distribution of Participants.

For military personnel only, what is your highest rank (category) achieved?

Life Satisfaction

Overall, life satisfaction was higher for military personnel than athletes. On a scale of zero though 10, zero being completely unsatisfied with life and 10 being completely satisfied with life, military personnel averaged 8.04 and athletes averaged 7.4. Table 4.6 summarizes individual's life satisfaction.

Table 4. 6: Life Satisfaction.

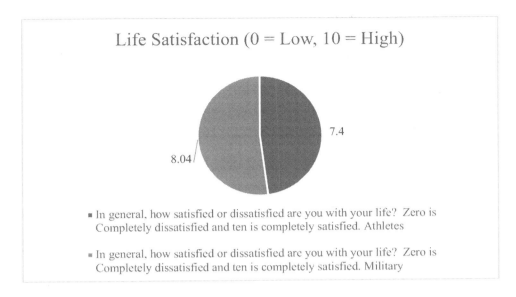

Life Satisfaction (0 = Low, 10 = High)

7.4

8.04

- In general, how satisfied or dissatisfied are you with your life? Zero is Completely dissatisfied and ten is completely satisfied. Athletes

- In general, how satisfied or dissatisfied are you with your life? Zero is Completely dissatisfied and ten is completely satisfied. Military

Education

Participants represented a varied range of education levels. The category with the highest level of education was the *completed college* category with a total of 16 individuals. *Some college* was next with a total of 11 individuals. The next category was *a graduate degree* with a total of eight. Table 4.7 summarizes the participant's educational level providing the percentage rating for each category.

Table 4. 7: Education Distribution of Participants.

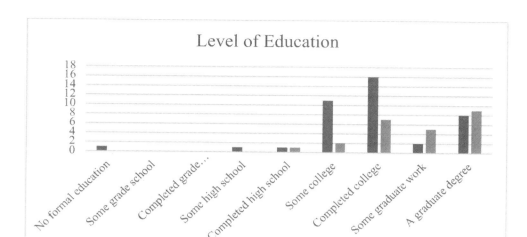

Descriptive Statistics

Descriptive statistics summarize quantitative data, enabling patterns and relationships to be discerned which were not readily apparent in raw data (Hussey & Hussey, 1997). Appendix (sport & Military leaders data appendix) contains the weighted average descriptive statistics for each item on the CBS-S where participants are responding on behalf of sport and military leaders. The weighted average is the mean computed with respect to the frequency of the values in a data set. When performing a *t-test* for all the weighted averages of the 47 items on the CBS-S comparing respondents of sport leaders versus respondents of military leaders, the *P*-value was 0.94, which indicates that the researcher has a 94% chance of finding a result less close to expectation and consequently a less than six percent chance of finding a result this close or closer. These findings suggest that coaching styles between sport and military leaders are reliably similar.

Results of the Correlation Analysis

As already mentioned, the hypotheses of this study were concerned with examining the similarities and differences in leadership styles between sport and military personnel. Using a *t-test*, the researcher investigated the relationship between sport leaders and military leaders. Five subgroups were divided into five research questions and a *P*-value was calculated to determine the probability of each category using similar coaching styles for sport and military leaders. A value closer to 1.0 represents a high positive relationship, and a lower value closer to or less than 0.05 represents a negative relationship. Coaching styles were determined measuring five categories from the CBS-S, physical training and planning, technical skills, mental preparation, goal setting, and personal rapport. This study also included a demographic gathering section.

Research Question 1

How do athletes and military personnel rate their leaders in physical training and planning?

Table 4. 8: Summary of Hypotheses for Research Question 1.

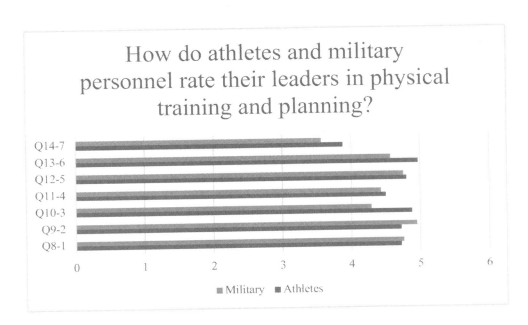

The data provided in Table 4.8 show the weighted averages for Questions 8-14 on the survey which correspond with questions 1-7 from the CBS-S instrument. When examining athletes and military personnel responses in the table, it is clear that all of the responses are similar, and thus there is a reasonable probability of similarity between sport and military leaders with respect to physical training and planning.

Research Question 2

How do athletes and military personnel rate their leaders in technical skills?

Table 4. 9: Summary of Hypotheses for Research Question 2.

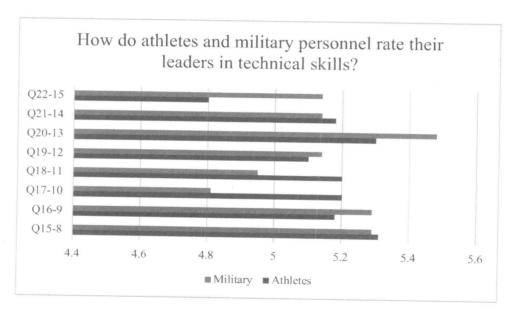

Table 4.9 shows the most similarity between sport and military leadership styles, this shows that further examination into how technical skills training is conducted is worth investigation. According to these findings, when examining the five categories of leadership style being examined in this study, technical skills training shows the most promise regarding an overlapping theme that may spread to additional industries.

Research Question 3

How do athletes and military personnel rate their leaders in mental preparation?

Table 4.10: Summary of Hypotheses for Research Question 3.

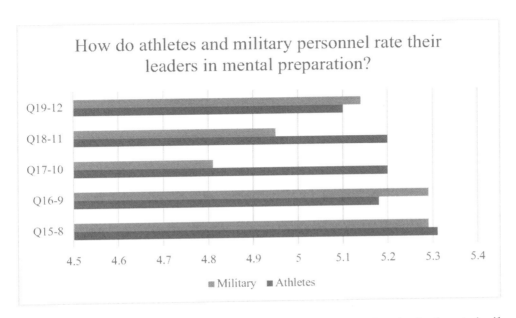

From Table 4.10, it is clear that mental preparation is the least similar category between sport and military leadership styles. Specifically, Question 10, "gives me reinforcement about correct technique," and 11, "provides me with feedback that helps me improve my technique" from the CBS-S seem to vary drastically. It may be of value in a future investigation to determine why sport and military leaders vary so much with regards to mental preparation, as well as which method is more successful regarding goal attainment.

Research Question 4

How do athletes and military personnel rate their leaders in goal setting?

Table 4. 11: Summary of Hypotheses for Research Question 4.

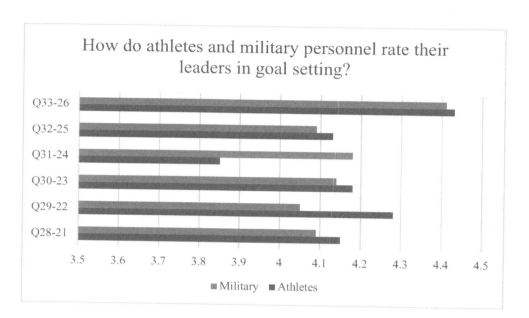

The data provided from Table 4.11 show the value of goal setting among sport and military leaders. Goal setting is invaluable to any organization. Regardless of institution, there is some version of goal setting whether it is referred to as a goal, vision, mission, dream, etc. For this reason, understanding effective goal setting styles is of value to leaders.

Research Question 5

How do athletes and military personnel rate their leaders in personal rapport?

Table 4. 12: Summary of Hypotheses for Research Question 5.

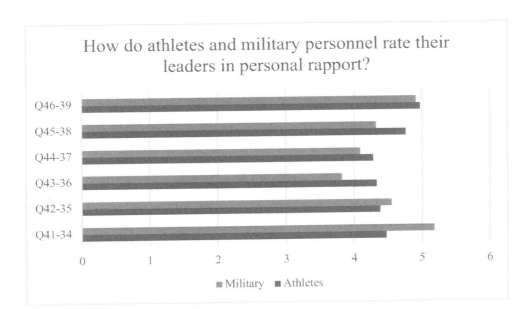

From Table 4.12, it is clear that establishing strong personal rapport is of value to sport and military leaders. When leaders and their followers establish a positive personal rapport, communicating will be more effective and the other four leadership styles being examined will be more effectively disseminated up and down communication channels.

CHAPTER V

CONCLUSIONS, DISCUSSION, AND RECOMMENDATIONS

In Chapter V, the researcher includes the purpose, implications of the findings, limitations, recommendations for future research, and the conclusion.

Purpose

The purpose of this study was to examine the similarities and differences in leadership styles between sport and military personnel. The researcher sought to discover the following: The relationship between sport and military leadership styles. The following research questions and hypotheses are presented once again to properly evaluate the problem.

RQ1: How do athletes and military personnel rate their leaders in physical training and planning?

Ho1: There is not a statistically significant difference between sport and military leadership styles as measured by physical training and planning

Ha1: There is a statistically significant difference between sport and military leadership styles as measured by physical training and planning

RQ2: How do athletes and military personnel rate their leaders in technical skills?

Ho2: There is not a statistically significant difference between sport and military leadership styles as measured by technical skills

Ha2: There is a statistically significant difference between sport and military leadership styles as measured by technical skills

RQ3: How do athletes and military personnel rate their leaders in mental preparation?

Ho3: There is not a statistically significant difference between sport and military leadership styles as measured by mental preparation

Ha3: There is a statistically significant difference between sport and military leadership styles as measured by mental preparation

RQ4: How do athletes and military personnel rate their leaders in goal setting?

Ho4: There is not a statistically significant difference between sport and military leadership styles as measured by goal setting

Ha4: There is a statistically significant difference between sport and military leadership styles as measured by goal setting

RQ5: How do athletes and military personnel rate their leaders in personal rapport?

Ho5: There is not a statistically significant difference between sport and military leadership styles as measured by personal rapport

Ha5: There is a statistically significant difference between sport and military leadership styles as measured by personal rapport

The findings of the study provide an important addition to the art of leadership and identify leadership styles that are common between two diverse and dynamic populations. This is of value to leaders since most industries are diversifying and operating faster and evolving more rapidly than during previous generations. These findings may be applicable to other diverse and dynamic institutions, for the reason sports and the military are so diverse and dynamic, including a wide range of racial, age, and gender diversity as well as an assortment of skills, knowledge, and experience among team members. If the researcher can identify common ground in such a large population, then the leadership styles may transfer to any industry.

The sample population consisted of 64 participants. The researcher posted his survey email to his Facebook and LinkedIn pages and relevant groups within those social networks as well as three group emails to athletes and military personnel asking if they know anyone including themselves willing to participate in the study. The researcher also created a blog post on the researcher's professional website www.improvewithchris.com, which was available to anyone meeting the participant qualifications. A total of 63 athletes and 30 military personnel responded, representing a range of sports and military branches, but only 64 total participants completed enough of the survey to provide value.

The researcher obtained the data and used correlations to analyze the data. The researcher then calculated the correlation of each category of the CBS-S. Ranking of most similar to least similar leadership styles between sport and military leaders were:

1. Technical skills with a *P*-value of 0.96

2. Goal setting with a *P*-value of 0.91

3. Personal Rapport with a *P*-value of 0.82

4. Training and Planning with a *P*-value of 0.47

5. Mental Preparation with a *P*-Value of 0.07

Implication of the Findings

Research Findings 1

How do athletes and military personnel rate their leaders in physical training and planning? The researcher's results showed there was a relationship between physical training and planning among sport and military leadership styles (P-value = 0.47). For hypotheses Ho1 and Ha1, the data provided showed that there was a positive correlation between physical training and planning styles during coaching when comparing sport and military leaders. The data provided that there is sufficient evidence at the alpha level of significance to support the claim that there is not a significant difference between sport and military leadership styles as measured by physical training and planning, the hypothesis was accepted.

Both sport and military leaders share similar leadership styles during physical training and planning. According to research, studies have shown there is a strong link between planning and project success (Serrador, 2012). The results of this study indicated that physical training and planning styles are similar in sports and the military.

Vince Lombardi once said, "fatigue makes cowards of us all (Jenkins, 2010)." When ample physical training and planning is conducted prior to a sports competition or military campaign, both athletes and military personnel will be better prepared for their opponents. The results of this study revealed that sport and military leaders have similar leadership styles when physically training and planning their people. Knowing this, an examination into how successful sports teams and military units physically and mentally prepare is worth further investigation and may better prepare individuals for obstacles and challenges.

Research Findings 2

How do athletes and military personnel rate their leaders in technical skills? Technical skill is a collection of actions required to perform a task. The researcher's results showed there was a relationship between technical skills training among sport and military leadership styles (P-value = 0.96). For hypotheses Ho2 and Ha2, the data provided showed that there was a strong positive correlation between technical skills styles during coaching when comparing sport and military leaders. The data provided that there is sufficient evidence at the alpha level of significance to support the claim that there is not a significant difference between sport and military leadership styles as measured by technical skills, the hypothesis was accepted.

Both sport and military leaders share similar leadership styles during technical skills training. According to research, studies have shown technical skills training is evolving to match the demands of the environment (Aggarwal & Darzi, 2006). What is not clear is how technical skills training should take place. By examining sport and military leaders, insight can be gathered into what leaders in these industries are doing which can be applied to other industries. The results of this study indicated that technical skills training styles are similar in sports and the military.

An individual's ability to perform his/her job is crucial to success. The New England Patriots have been to eight Super Bowls in 14 years under the leadership of head coach Bill Belichick. Coach Belichick has a philosophy he never strays from, "do your job!" Do your job can translate to mean that every person on the team takes the time to master and perform their technical skills and when everyone does this, the team as a whole comes together and performs exceptionally (Kerr, 2015).

Research Findings 3

How do athletes and military personnel rate their leaders in mental preparation? It has been said that, "to attain peak performance in sports competitions, coaches and athletes should not base their prospect on physical training on sport skills alone rather should integrate both the mental and physical aspects of performance" (Ohuruogu, Jonathan, & Ikeckukwu, 2016). At times, leaders can become too caught up in the physical or technical performance metrics and forget the importance of mental preparation. The researcher's results showed there was a relationship between mental preparation among sport and military leadership styles (P-value = 0.07). For hypotheses Ho3 and Ha3, the data provided showed that there was a positive correlation between mental preparation styles during coaching when comparing sport and military leaders. The data provided that there is sufficient evidence at the alpha level of significance to support the claim that there is not a significant difference between sport and military leadership styles as measured by mental preparation, the hypothesis was accepted.

Both sport and military leaders share similar leadership styles during mental preparation training. "Every quarterback can throw a ball; every running back can run; every receiver is fast; but that mental toughness that you talk about translates into competitiveness." – Tom Brady (Middleton, 2016). The results of this study indicated that mental preparation training styles are similar in sports and the military.

Research Findings 4

How do athletes and military personnel rate their leaders in goal setting? In order to create effective plans, there must be a goal that those plans are aimed to achieve. "Goal setting is the process of establishing an outcome (a goal) to serve as the aim of one's actions" (Turkay, 2014). Goals provide direction. Without clear and concise goals, a leader's team is left wondering what to do and how to do it. Goals provide a basis for developing a plan. Once a goal is in place, a plan can be developed to achieve that goal. The researcher's results showed there was a relationship between goal setting among sport and military leadership styles (P-value = 0.91). For hypotheses Ho4 and Ha4, the data provided showed that there was a strong positive correlation between mental preparation styles during coaching when comparing sport and military leaders. The data provided that there is sufficient evidence at the alpha level of significance to support the claim that there is not a significant difference between sport and military leadership styles as measured by goal setting, the hypothesis was accepted.

Beyond the main goal, smaller goals should be established as checkpoints along the way. It is often noted that goals should be S.M.A.R.T. Specific, measurable, attainable, relevant, and timely. Specific goals are clear and concise. They get the point across with little room for misinterpretation. Measurable goals have a quantitative method of measuring progress. Attainable goals are goals which are realistic for the leader and the team. Relevant goals are goals which progress towards the overarching objective. Finally, time bound goals are those that have a deadline, so their progress can be measured over a period. The results of this study indicated that goal setting styles are similar in sports and the military.

Research Findings 5

How do athletes and military personnel rate their leaders in personal rapport? Personal rapport is the basic ability to get along with others. It should not take scientific research to determine that leaders who do not get along with their teams will be less effective than leaders who establish a positive personal rapport with their team. With that said, a study by Duchan and Kovarsky (2011) identified rapport as an ongoing process of meaning-making that is a co-constructed and interactive part of communication. One aspect of leadership is opening communication channels within a team in order to create novel ideas to overcome obstacles. When a leader establishes a strong personal rapport with their team, it enhances communication and encourages idea cultivation. The researcher's results showed there was a relationship between establishing personal rapport among sport and military leadership styles (P-value = 0.82). For hypotheses Ho5 and Ha5, the data provided showed that there was a strong positive correlation between mental preparation styles during coaching when comparing sport and military leaders. The data provided that there is sufficient evidence at the alpha level of significance to support the claim that there is not a significant difference between sport and military leadership styles as measured by personal rapport, the hypothesis was accepted.

As mentioned in Chapter II's review of research, Joo et al., (2012) learned creativity has a significant relationship between perceived learning cultures. In return, creativity also enhanced team cohesion, which adds to support structure, acting as a full circle feedback system with team creativity. Creativity is what allows people to learn how to become leaders after initially failing. Kim, Magnusen, and Andrew (2016) proposed that horizontal communication had a significant positive association with both group integration-task and group integration-social meaning. When people in a group accepted each other, they had a higher incidence of team cohesion. Alternatively, when teams did not accept each other they did not work together as well. People need to be able to work effectively together if they are to get the most creativity out of their projects. Coming together to create something better than what can be achieved alone is common throughout all of human history. This extract from chapter two is a reminder of the importance of communication and establishing personal rapport for team cohesiveness. The results of this study indicated that styles used to establish personal rapport are similar in sports and the military.

These findings imply that the common characteristics of sport leaders and the common characteristics of military leaders identified in Chapter II's literature review overlap when applied to the five areas examined using the CBS-S. Those findings show a relationship between the leadership characteristics common between sport and military leaders when applying them to the five categories examined in the study.

Table 5. 1: Chance of Finding a Result less Close to Expectation.

Technical skills 96%
Goal setting 91%
Personal Rapport 82%
Training and Planning 47%
Mental Preparation 7%

Table 5. 2: Leadership Characteristics Common Between Sport & Military Leaders.

Professional Excellence: Competence in Team Building, Self-Efficacy, High Performance Standard, Shared Knowledge, Coordination, Interconnected, Courageous Enough to Pursue the Right Cause, Empowering Subordinates, Transformational Leadership, Leads by Example
Positive Personality Traits: Physical Prowess – Ability, High Work Ethic, Determination, Motivation, Autocratic / Authoritative Behavior, Focus on Training and Instruction
Team Cohesion: Collective Efficacy, Team Mental Models, Sense of Responsibility, Motivation, Support, Communication
Well-Balanced Vision: Letting go of Values that no Longer Serve, Managing Present Values, Creating and Adopting New Values
Empathy: Impeccable Moral Integrity, Genuine Concern for Command, Self-Sacrifice for Subordinates, Sincerity of Purpose, Compassionate Approach Towards all in General

Limitations

The findings of this study have certain limitations. One limitation could be that the representatives of sport and military leaders may not accurately represent leaders from other industries. Although the fields of sport and the military are diverse and dynamic areas, representing a wide range of leadership styles, it is impossible to capture every aspect of a leader.

Another limitation is representatives of sport and military personnel may provide a description of their leader that differs significantly from how others view the same leader. Perceptions and experiences vary between individuals and these variations can lead to different outcomes during the survey regarding the same leader.

A third limitation is the degree to which the participants understand the questions. Although the CBS-S survey instrument and demographic survey were explained in the beginning of the questionnaire and participants were notified to contact the researcher if they had any questions, interpretations can vary. An individual may think he/she understands a question but not fully grasp it or be interpreting the question differently than anticipated.

A final limitation is respondents of the study may not have answered honestly while evaluating their coach or supervisor without fear of repercussions from above. Although it was outlined in the consent form that the survey is unanimous, some individuals may not answer honestly in fear that their supervisor will discover they are responding in a way that may interfere with their career.

Recommendations for Future Research

These findings are just the beginning, this research has discovered that there are similarities in multiple aspects of leadership styles between sport and military leaders. These findings do not indicate how the five areas, physical training and planning, technical skills, mental preparation, goal setting, and personal rapport should be conducted. This research was meant to identify leadership styles that have shown promise in today's fast-paced and constantly changing environment. Future research should investigate different ideas and methods of executing all of these areas of leadership. "People who have combined their leadership style with strategic ideas and plans are far more likely to achieve the results they desire because it is a person's fundamental behaviors and frame of mind that brings strategy, goals, and plans to life" (Stowell & Mead, 2016).

The research has also identified the order in which the aspects of leadership are most similar and least similar between sport and the military and are in order from most to least similar, technical skills, goal setting, personal rapport, training and planning, and mental preparation. This order does not imply what makes these aspects more or less similar, just which leadership styles are more similar between sport and military leaders. Further research could investigate what specifically is similar between these aspects of leadership style.

Finally, the relationship identified between the five areas explored during the research study allowed a new relationship to be made, linking leadership characteristics between sport and military leaders from Chapter II's literature review. This relationship provides reason to explore how those leadership characteristics are being used by sport and military leaders in the five areas explored during this study and teach those findings to leaders.

Conclusion

The main objective of the study was to examine the similarities and differences in leadership styles between sport and military personnel. Evidence supported the reliability and validity of the CBS-S measurement instrument.

As part of this dissertation study, the previous chapter presented the data derived from 40 athletes and 24 military personnel. Along with descriptive statistics and reliability analysis, empirical results of the research were presented. The researcher presents the following significant results:

1. There is not a significant difference between sport and military leadership styles as measured by physical training and planning.

2. There is not a significant difference between sport and military leadership styles as measured by technical skills.

3. There is not a significant difference between sport and military leadership styles as measured by mental preparation.

4. There is not a significant difference between sport and military leadership styles as measured by goal setting.

5. There is not a significant difference between sport and military leadership styles as measured by personal rapport.

The results of the study revealed that sport leadership styles had a positive correlation with military leadership styles. This means that leadership styles which involve physical training and planning, technical skills, mental preparation, goal setting, and personal rapport can look to what successful sport leaders and military leaders are doing for guidance. This statement is based on the concept that the styles are similar and already working in multiple industries, therefore they may be applicable to additional industries such as medicine, education, government, technology, science, and profit and non-profit.

Regardless of industry, there is always a focus on technical skills training. All members of a group must be able to properly execute their task, or they will bring the group down. Knowing this, the results of this study revealed a strong positive correlation between sport and military leadership styles with respect to technical skills training based on P-values. The P-values were 0.96, therefore the researcher failed to reject the null hypothesis. This means that the leadership styles which involve technical skills training are very similar among sport and military leaders and a further examination into how successful sport and military leaders teach technical skills would be a great value to leaders.

This present study provides another insight into the diverse and dynamic field of leadership by examining two large, diverse, and dynamic industries. Hopefully, this study provides a starting point and direction for the future development of leaders. The world in which today's leaders operate is fast-pace and always changing. If the art of leadership wants to keep up, it must evolve to match its environment. Perhaps these findings can provide leaders with a map to navigate through this face-paced and always changing discipline.

REFERENCES

Adair, J. E. (1973). *Action centered leadership.* London, England: McGraw-Hill.

Aggarwal, R., & Darzi, A. (2006). Technical-skills training in the 21st century. *The New England Journal of Medicine, 355:*2695-2696. DOI: 10.1056/NEJMME068179

Bandura, A. (1997). *Self-efficacy: The exercise of control.* New York: W. H. Freeman.

Bangari, R. S. (2014). Establishing a framework of transformational grassroots military leadership: Lessons from high-intensity, high-risk operational environments. *Vikalpa: Journal of Decision Makers, 39*(3), 13-34.

Bangari, R. S., & Prasad, L. (2012). Leadership in action: Courage, the critical leadership differentiator. *ASCI Journal of Management, 41*(2), 40-75.

Bjorn, P., & Ngwenyama, O. (2008). Virtual team collaboration: Building shared meaning, resolving breakdowns and creating translucence. *Information Systems Journal, 19*(3), 225-339.

Boies, K., & Howell, J. M. (2009). Leading military teams to think and feel: Exploring the relationship between leadership, soldiers' cognitive and affective process, and team effectiveness. *Military Psychology, 21*(2), 216-232.

Bourjade, M., Thierry, B., Hausberger, M., & Petit, O. (2015). Is leadership a reliable concept in animals? An empirical study in the horse. *PLoS ONE, 10*(5), 1-4.

Burton, R. (2010, March 13). The author of 'Red Badge' loved the game more than his studies. *New York Times.* Retrieved from http://www.nytimes.com/2010/03/14/sports/ baseball/14crane.html

Caron, J. G., Bloom, G. A., Loughead, T. M., & Hoffman, M. D. (2016). Paralympic athlete leaders' perceptions of leadership and cohesion. *Journal of Sport Behavior, 39*(3), 219-20.

Chartrand, T. L., & Bargh, J. A. (1999). The chameleon effect: The perception-behavior link and social interaction. *Journal of Personality and Social Psychology, 76*(6), 893-910.

Coletta, S. L. (2012). Fix it as best you can, and learn from your mistakes: Apology lessons, past and present. *Frontiers of Health Services Management, 28*(3), 36-41.

Collinson, D., & Tourish, D. (2015). Teaching leadership critically: New directions for leadership pedagogy. *Academy of Management Learning & Education, 14*(4), 576-594.

Cormier, M. L., Bloom, G. A., & Harvey, W. J. (2015). Elite coach perceptions of coaching teams. *International Journal of Sports Science & Coaching, 10*(6), 1039.

Dalenberg, S., Vogelaar, A. L. W., & Beersma, B. (2009). The effect of a team strategy discussion on military team performance. *Military Psychology, 2,* 31-46.

Department of The Army. (1997). *The Officer/ NCO Relationship.*

Department of the Army. (2001). *Operations FM 3-0.*

Department of the Army. (2012). *Army Leadership ADRP 6-22.*

Duchan, J. F., & Kovarsky, D. (2011). Rapport and relationships in clinical interactions. *Topics in Language Disorders*, 31(4), 297- 299.

Edmundson, M. (2015). *Why football matters: My education in the game.* New York, NY: Penguin Books.

Eskridge, B. E., Vale, E., & Schlupp, I. (2015). Emergence of leadership within a homogeneous group. *PLOS ONE, 10*(7), e0134222. doi: 10.1371/journal.pone.0134222.

Fast, A., & Jensen, D. (2006). The NFL coaching network: Analysis of social network among professional football coaches. *American Association for Artificial Intelligence.* Retrieved from http://www.aaai.org/Papers/Symposia/Fall/2006/FS-06-02/FS06-02-017.pdf

Filho, E., Tenenbaum, G., & Yang, Y. (2015). Cohesion, team mental models, and collective efficacy: Towards an integrated framework of team dynamics in sport. *Journal of Sports Sciences, 33*(6), 641.

Fried, G. (2015). History and future of sport and public assembly facilities. In Park, A., *Managing Sport Facilities* (3rd ed.). (p. 12). Champaign, IL: Human Kinetics.

Gibbons, S. L., & Ebbeck, V. (2011). Team building through physical challenges in gender-segregated classes and student self-conceptions. *Journal of Experimental Education, 34*(1), 71-86.

Govindarajan, V., & Faber, H. (2016). To win the Civil War, Lincoln had to change his leadership. *Harvard Business Review Digital Articles,* 2-5.

Harris, N. (2016). Leadership development: An examination of the influence of sports experiences on leadership development of former female collegiate athletes (Doctoral dissertation, University of LaVerne). Retrieved from http://proxy.ussa.edu:2053/dissertations/docview/1785853070/D48 5B4CC84FC4A80PQ/3?accountid=29017

Harrison, H., & Smith, A. (2016). Careers and culture in sport and the military. *Sport & Exercise Specialist, 48*, 282.

Healy, A. (2015, December). Ranking NFL head coaches by strategic decision-making. *Inside.* Retrieved from http://www.espn.com/nfl/insider/story/_/id/14321399/ranking-nfl- head-coaches-strategic-decision-making

Hedges, C. (2002). *War is a force that gives us meaning.* New York, NY: Public Affairs.

Humphreys, B. R., & Humphreys, B. R. (2008). The size and scope of the sports industry in the United States. *International Association of Sports Economists, 8*(11).

Hussey, J., & Hussey, R. (1997). *Business Research: A Practical Guide for Undergraduate and Postgraduate Students.* London:Macmillan Press Ltd.

Inside Quest (Producer). (2016). *The Millennial Question.* [Simon Sinek]. Available from https://youtu.be/vudaAYx2IcE

James, W. (2015). *The moral equivalent of war.* Worcestershire, England: Read Books Ltd.

Jeffrey, C. (2012). *A functional model of team leadership for sport* (Doctoral Dissertation, Florida State University). Retrieved from http://proxy.ussa.edu:2053/docview/1035147832/E74874CAA633 4D02PQ/18?accountid=29017

Jenkins, S. (2010). *Vince Lombardi: The coach that still matters 40 years after his death.* The Washington Post.

Johnson-Laird, P. N. (1983). *Mental models: Towards a cognitive science of language, inference, and consciousness 6.* Cambridge, MA: Harvard University Press.

Jonathan, D. P. (2003). Can leadership be taught? Perspectives from management educators. *ACAD MANAG LEARN EDU. 2*(1), 54-67.

Joo, B., Song, J., Lim, D., & Yoon, S. (2012). Team creativity: The effects of perceived learning culture developmental feedback and team cohesion. *International Journal of Training & Development, 16*(2), 77-91.

Katz, R. L. (1955). Skills of an effective administrator. *Harvard Business Review, 33*(1), 33-42.

Kerr, J. (2015, January 26). How Bill Belichick's 'do your job' mantra applies to leadership. Retrieved from inc.com

Kim, S., Magnusen, M., & Andrew, D. P. S. (2016). Divided we fall: Examining the relationship between horizontal team communication and team commitment via team cohesion. *International Journal of Sports Science & Coaching, 11*(5), 625.

Maddux, J. E. (2002). Self-efficacy: The power of believing you can. In C. R. Snyder & S. Lopez (Eds.), *Handbook of positive psychology* (pp. 257–276). Oxford, UK: Oxford University Press.

Maneuver Self Study Program. (n. d.). In *U.S. Army Maneuver Center of Excellence (MCoE)*. Retrieved from

http://www.benning.army.mil/mssp/Military%20Leadership/

Marlantes, K. (2011). *What it is like to go to war.* New York, NY: Atlantic Monthly Press.

McKay, B. (Producer). (2013, May 20). *Mastery with Robert Greene.* [Audio podcast]. Retrieved from http://www.artofmanliness.com/2013/05/20/art-of-manliness-podcast-46-mastery-with-robert-greene/

McKay, B. (Producer). (2016, December 15). *Solitude, friendship, and how not to be an excellent sheep.* [Audio podcast]. Retrieved from http://www.artofmanliness.com/2016/12/15/podcast-261-solitude-friendship-can-make- better-leader/

McKay, B., & McKay, K. (Producers). (2014, June 14). *The charisma myth with Olivia Fox.* [Audio podcast]. Retrieved from http://www.artofmanliness.com/2014/06/14/art-of-manliness-podcast-72-the-charisma-myth-with-olivia-fox/

Middleton, Y. (2016, March 3). *46 phenomenal Tom Brady quotes.* Retrieved from addicted2success.com

Minniti, M., & Bygrave, W. (2001). A dynamic model of entrepreneurial learning. *Entrepreneurship: Theory and Practice, Spring.*

Mishra, T., Parra, P. G., & Abeel, T. (2014). The upside of failure: How regional student groups learn from their mistakes. *PLoS Computational Biology, 10*(8), 1- 3.

Mohammadzade, Y., Zardoshtaians, S., & Hossini, R. N. S. (2012). The relationship between leadership styles of coaches with motivational climate of Iranian elite male volleyball players. *International Journal of Academic Research in Business and SocialSciences. 2*(1).

Morath, R. A., Leonard, A. L., & Zaccaro, S. J. (2011). Military leadership: An overview and introduction to the special issue. *Military Psychology, 23*(5), 453-461.

Nicolosi, G., & Peng, L. (2008). Do individual investors learn from their trading experience? *Journal of Financial Markets, 12*(2), 317-336.

Northouse, P. G. (2013). *Leadership: Theory and practice (*6th ed.*).* Thousand Oaks, California: SAGE Publications.

Ohurougu, B., Jonathan, U., & Ikechukwu, U. (2016). Psychological preparation for peak performance in sports competition. *Journal of Education and Practice, 7(12).*

Page, A. N. (2004). Why smart executives fail and what you can learn from their mistakes/Why smart people can be so stupid. *Journal of Business Communication, 41*(4), 411- 416.

Rhodan, M. (2016, November). President Obama: Look to veterans for hope 'whenever the world makes you cynical.' *Time Magazine.* Retrieved from http://time.com/4568093/president-obama-veterans- hope/?xid=homepage

Ruggieri, S. (2013). Leadership style, self-sacrifice, and team identification. *Social Behavior and Personality, 41*(7).

Ryan, B. (2005, November 21). Belichick learned well from dad. *Boston Globe.*

    Retrieved from http://archive.boston.com/sports/football/patriots/articles/

    2005/11/21belichick_learned_well_from_dad/?page=full

Salvatore, N. (2014). Sport collaboration as a tool in cultural diversity. *Ovidius*

    University Annals, Series Physical Education & Sport/Science, Movement &

    Health, Supplement, 500.

Serrador, P. (2012). *The importance of the planning phase to project success.* Paper

    presented at PMI® Global Congress 2012—North America, Vancouver, British

    Columbia, Canada. Newtown Square, PA: Project Management Institute.

Shermer, M. (2008, December). Patternicicty: Finding meaningful patterns in

    meaningless   noise. *Scientific America,* retrieved from

    https://www.scientificamerican.com/article/patternicity-finding-meaningful-

    patterns/

Shiperd, A. M., Basevitch, I., Renner, K. B., & Siwatu, K. O. (2014).   Development

    and evaluation of a team building intervention with a U.S. collegiate rugby team:

    A mixed methods approach. *Journal of Multidisciplinary Research, 6*(2), 31-48.

Stark, S. (2010, September). Drill and kill: How Americans link war and sports.

    Atlantic. Retrieved from

http://www.theatlantic.com/entertainment/archive/2010/09/drill-and-kill-how-americans-

    link-war-and-sports/63832/

Stowell, S., & Mead, S. (2016). *The art of strategic leadership: How leaders at all levels*

    prepare themselves, their teams, and organizations for the future. Hoboken, NJ:

    John Wiley & Sons, Inc.

Taylor, S. (2014, March). Sport and the decline of war. *Psychology Today.* Retrieved from https://www.psychologytoday.com/blog/out-the-darkness/201403/sport-and-the-decline-war

TED-Ed (Producer). (2016). *How do schools of fish swim in harmony - Nathan S. Jacobs.* [TED-Ed]. Available from http://ed.ted.com/lessons/how-do-schools-of-fish-swim-in-harmony-nathan-s-jacobs.

Tillman, B. (2015). 'The big e' leadership factory. *Naval History, 29*(4), 16-21.

Turkay, S. (2014). *Setting goals: Who, why, how?* Manuscript. Retrieved from https://hilt.harvard.edu/files/hilt/files/settinggoals.pdf

Ucbasaran, D., Shepherd, D. A., Lockett, A., & Lyon, S. J. (2012). Life after business failure for entrepreneurs. *Journal of Management, 39*(1), 163-202.

Webb, C. (2016). How small shifts in leadership can transform your team dynamic. *McKinsey Quarterly, 2*, 74-81.

Xiang, W., Sun, L., Chen, S., Yang, Z., & Liu, Z. (2015). The role of mental models in collaborative sketching. *International Journal of Technology & Design Education, 25*(1), 121-136.

APPENDICES

APPENDIX A

Informed Consent Form

The purpose of this study is to examine sport and military leaders for universal leadership characteristics that spread across industries.

For this project, you will be asked to participate in one survey which will be limited to a maximum of fifteen minutes. If necessary, a follow-up email may be requested for clarification purposes.

All data will be maintained as confidential and no identifying information such as your name or your place of work will appear in any publication or presentation of the data.

There are no foreseeable risks or ill effects anticipated from participating in this study. One benefit you may gain from your participation in this study is a chance to help future leaders learn from current leaders.

Your participation in this study is completely voluntary and you are free to withdraw from the study at any time for any reason without penalty or prejudice from the investigator. Please feel free to ask any questions of the investigator before signing the Informed Consent Form or at any time during the study.

I, _____, agree to participate in this research project entitled, "Universal Leadership Characteristics." The study has been explained to me and my questions have been answered to my satisfaction. I have read the description of this project and give consent to participate.

Participant's Signature   Date

_____   _____

Principal Investigator:

Christopher P. Johnson, Doctoral Student

United States Sports Academy

One Academy Drive

Daphne Al 36526

Faculty Supervisor:

Dr. Bret Simmermacher

(251) 626-3303

APPENDIX B

Letter to Prospect Participants

Colleagues and friends,

As some of you may know, I am currently performing research on my dissertation to complete my doctoral program. If any of you are or know of someone else who is an athlete or military personnel who fits the below guidelines and is willing to partake in my study attempting to gain better insight into team leadership, please respond to this message.

Athlete: Currently or previously participated in sport under a coach's guidance.

Military Personnel: Currently or previously been a member of the United States Military.

Thank you very much for your time and assistance, my hope is that together we can make tomorrow better by educating future leaders today.

Very respectfully,

Christopher P. Johnson, Doctoral Student

Principal Investigator

United States Sports Academy, One Academy Drive, Daphne Al 36526

APPENDIX C

Demographic Questionnaire

This interview is being conducted as a part of my dissertation research of sport and military leadership. You have received a consent form to sign, which indicates your consent to this interview.

1. Are you filling out this survey as an athlete or military personnel (select one)?

      Athlete

      Military Personnel

2. What is your age?

      <18

      19-29

      30-39

      40-49

      50-59

      60-69

      70-79

      80+

3. For athletes only, what is your primary sport (Select one)?

American Football

American Soccer

Badminton

Baseball

Basketball

Cross Country

Field Hockey

Lacrosse

Softball

Swimming

Tennis

Track & Field

Volleyball

Wrestling

Other

4. For military personnel only, which branch are you associated with?

Air Force

Army

Coast Guard

Marine Corps

Navy

5. For military personnel only, what is your highest rank achieved?

Junior Enlisted

Senior Enlisted (NCO)

Warrant Officer

Commissioned Officer

6. In general, how satisfied or dissatisfied are you with your life?

1 completed satisfied

2 mostly satisfied

3 neither satisfied nor dissatisfied

4 mostly dissatisfied

5 completely dissatisfied

7. What is your highest level of education

      1 no formal education

      2 some grade school

      3 completed grade school

      4 some high school

      5 completed high school

      6 some college

      7 completed college

      8 some graduate work

9 a graduate degree

APPENDIX D

Coaching Behaviour Scale for Sport (CBS-S)

COACHING BEHAVIOUR SCALE for SPORT (CBS-S©)

HOW FREQUENTLY DO YOU EXPERIENCE THE FOLLOWING COACHING BEHAVIOURS

Some athletes have a single coach and others work with a coaching team. If you have more than one coach, think of the coach, or coaches, most responsible for that area.

Please use the scale below to answer all the sections.

1	2	3	4	5	6	7
Never	Rarely	Sometimes	Fairly often	Often	Very often	Always

The coach(es) most responsible for my physical training and conditioning.....

	Never			Fairly often			Always
1. provides me with a physical conditioning program in which I am confident.	1	2	3	4	5	6	7
2. provides me with a physically challenging conditioning program.	1	2	3	4	5	6	7
3. provides me with a detailed physical conditioning program.	1	2	3	4	5	6	7
4. provides me with a plan for my physical preparation.	1	2	3	4	5	6	7
5. ensures that training facilities and equipment are organized.	1	2	3	4	5	6	7
6. provides me with structured training sessions.	1	2	3	4	5	6	7
7. provides me with an annual training program.	1	2	3	4	5	6	7

The coach(es) most responsible for my technical skills.....

	Never			Fairly often			Always
8. provides me with advice while I'm performing a skill.	1	2	3	4	5	6	7
9. gives me specific feedback for correcting technical errors.	1	2	3	4	5	6	7
10. gives me reinforcement about correct technique.	1	2	3	4	5	6	7
11. provides me with feedback that helps me improve my technique.	1	2	3	4	5	6	7
12. provides visual examples to show how a skill should be done.	1	2	3	4	5	6	7
13. uses verbal examples that describe how a skill should be done.	1	2	3	4	5	6	7
14. makes sure I understand the techniques and strategies I'm being taught.	1	2	3	4	5	6	7
15. provides me with immediate feedback.	1	2	3	4	5	6	7

The coach(es) most responsible for my mental preparation.....

	Never			Fairly often			Always
16. provides advice on how to perform under pressure.	1	2	3	4	5	6	7
17. provides advice on how to be mentally tough.	1	2	3	4	5	6	7
18. provides advice on how to stay confident about my abilities.	1	2	3	4	5	6	7
19. provides advice on how to stay positive about myself.	1	2	3	4	5	6	7
20. provides advice on how to stay focused.	1	2	3	4	5	6	7

The coach(es) most responsible for my goal setting.....

	Never			Fairly often			Always
21. helps me identify strategies to achieve my goals.	1	2	3	4	5	6	7
22. monitors my progress toward my goals.	1	2	3	4	5	6	7
23. helps me set-short term goals.	1	2	3	4	5	6	7
24. helps me identify target dates for attaining my goals.	1	2	3	4	5	6	7
25. helps me set long-term goals.	1	2	3	4	5	6	7

						CBS-S©	
26. provides support to attain my goals.	1	2	3	4	5	6	7

The coach(es) most responsible for my <u>competition strategies</u>…..

	Never			Fairly often			Always
27. helps me focus on the process of performing well	1	2	3	4	5	6	7
28. prepares me to face a variety of situations in competition.	1	2	3	4	5	6	7
29. keeps me focused in competitions.	1	2	3	4	5	6	7
30. has a consistent routine at competition.	1	2	3	4	5	6	7
31. deals with problems I may experience at competitions.	1	2	3	4	5	6	7
32. shows confidence in my ability during competitions.	1	2	3	4	5	6	7
33. ensures that facilities and equipment are organized for competition.	1	2	3	4	5	6	7

My head coach…..

	Never			Fairly often			Always
34. shows understanding for me as a person.	1	2	3	4	5	6	7
35. is a good listener.	1	2	3	4	5	6	7
36. is easily approachable about personal problems I might have.	1	2	3	4	5	6	7
37. demonstrates concern for my whole self (i.e., other parts of my life than sport).	1	2	3	4	5	6	7
38. is trustworthy with my personal problems.	1	2	3	4	5	6	7
39. maintains confidentiality regarding my personal life.	1	2	3	4	5	6	7
40. uses fear in his/her coaching methods.	1	2	3	4	5	6	7
41. yells at me when angry.	1	2	3	4	5	6	7
42. disregards my opinion.	1	2	3	4	5	6	7
43. shows favoritism towards others.	1	2	3	4	5	6	7
44. intimidates me physically.	1	2	3	4	5	6	7
45. uses power to manipulate me.	1	2	3	4	5	6	7
46. makes personal comments to me that I find upsetting.	1	2	3	4	5	6	7
47. spends more time coaching the best athletes	1	2	3	4	5	6	7

CBS-S©

Note for Researchers

- The CBS-S has 47 items divided into 7 different constructs

    1. Physical training and planning -   Items 1-7
    2. Technical skills -   Items 8-15
    3. Mental preparation   Items 16-20
    4. Goal setting -   Items 21-26
    5. Competition strategies -   Items 27-33
    6. Personal rapport -   Items 34-39
    7. Negative personal rapport -   Items 40-47

- References

Côté, J., Yardley, J., Hay, J., Sedgwick, W., & Baker, J. (1999). An exploratory examination of the Coaching Behavior Scale for Sport, *AVANTE. 5*, 82-92.

Baker, J. R., Côté, J., & Hawes, R. A. (2000). The relationship between coaching behaviours and sport anxiety. *Journal of Science and Medicine in Sport, 3 (2)*, 110-119.

Baker, J., Yardley, J., & Côté, J. (2003). Coach behaviors and athlete satisfaction in team and individual sports. *International Journal of Sport Psychology. 34*, 226-239.

Sullivan, P.J., Bloom, G.A., & Falcao, W.R. (2014). A confirmatory factor analysis of the Coach Behavior Scale for Sport. *Journal of Sport Behavior, 37*, 190-202.

- For more information regarding the CBS-S please contact

Jean Côté, Ph.D.
Professor
School of Kinesiology and Health Studies
Kingston, Ontario, Canada
K7L 3N6
Phone: (613) 533-6000 X 79049
E-mail: jc46@queensu.ca

APPENDIX E

Thank You Note

Respondents, thank you for taking time to respond to this survey. Your participation is greatly appreciated and the information you have provided will serve only the intended purpose of future leader development.

Sincerely,

Christopher P. Johnson

cpjohnson@students.ussa.edu

Appendix F

Sport & Military Leader Data

CBS-S Questions (Q1-Q7 were demographic questions)	Sports Leader Weighted Averages	Military Leader Weighted Averages
Q8-1	4.72	4.76
Q9-2	4.72	4.95
Q10-3	4.88	4.29
Q11-4	4.5	4.43
Q12-5	4.8	4.76
Q13-6	4.97	4.57
Q14-7	3.88	3.57
Q15-8	5.31	5.29
Q16-9	5.18	5.29
Q17-10	5.2	4.81
Q18-11	5.2	4.95
Q19-12	5.1	5.14
Q20-13	5.3	5.48
Q21-14	5.18	5.14
Q22-15	4.8	5.14
Q23-16	4.18	4.82
Q24-17	4.41	4.77
Q25-18	4.18	4.86
Q26-19	4.33	4.18
Q27-20	4.33	4.32
Q28-21	4.15	4.09
Q29-22	4.28	4.05
Q30-23	4.18	4.14
Q31-24	3.85	4.18
Q32-25	4.13	4.09
Q33-26	4.43	4.41
Q34-27	4.8	4.82
Q35-28	4.7	5.05
Q36-29	4.93	4.59
Q37-30	4.93	4.64
Q38-31	4.78	4.36
Q39-32	5.05	5.23
Q40-33	4.85	5.09
Q41-34	4.47	5.18
Q42-35	4.38	4.55
Q43-36	4.33	3.82
Q44-37	4.28	4.09
Q45-38	4.76	4.32
Q46-39	4.97	4.91
Q47-40	2.44	3.36
Q48-41	2.76	3.23
Q49-42	2.63	2.64
Q50-43	3.77	3.09
Q51-44	1.41	1.59
Q52-45	1.72	1.59
Q53-46	2.05	1.55
Q54-47	3.21	2.55

Appendix G
IRB Approval

g. Has this study been rejected by another IRB, similar review board, departmental committee(s), thesis/dissertation committee? Yes ☐ No ☑

If YES – Give the reasons: _____

Note: If the protocol has/is subsequently rejected or disapproved by another review board, the USSA IRB Committee must be notified promptly.

Check the relevant review items below and check for included copies, as part of the application.

Check	Item	Dates
☑	1. This application.	
☑	2. Application must have original PI signatures.	
☑	3. Informed Consent and Assent Forms, fact or information sheets; include phone and verbal consent scripts. HIPAA authorization addendum to consent form.	
☑	4. All recruitment materials including scripts, flyers and advertising, letters, emails. Focus group guides, scripts used to guide phone or in-person interviews, etc.	
☑	5. Complete copy of Methods with complete copy of List of Equipment utilized, Questionnaire & Survey.	
☑	6. Documentation of reviews from any other committees (e.g., Research, Dissertation Committee or Thesis Committee, or local review committees in Academic Affairs).	
☑	7. Complete copy of Research Design, Dissertation/Thesis Proposal, Chapters I, II, & III with all Appendices --- as it is applicable.	
☑	8. Copy of the Approval Sheet with Committee Signatures & Comment	
☑	9. Benefits of Study Statement / Statement of Purpose / Significance of Study	

Decision based upon Review: ACCEPTED ☑   NOT ACCEPTED ☐

IRB Committee Member Name: _FRED J. Cromartie_
                                                         (Print)

IRB Committee Member Signature: _____

Made in the USA
Middletown, DE
27 July 2018